To _____

God loves you and I love you.

From _____

WILD SIDE PUBLISHING
Auckland, New Zealand
www.wildsidepublishing.com

ISBN Soft cover 978-1-991299-71-0

Unless otherwise noted, all Scripture is taken from the New International Version®, NIV®. Copyright © 1973, 1978, 1984, 2011 by Biblica, Inc.™ Used by permission of Zondervan. All rights reserved worldwide.

Design by Ruth Riding

Typeset in Daisy Avenue and Rockwell

Cataloguing in Publishing Data
  Title: Switched On
  Author: Sharline Aldridge
  Subjects: Children's discipleship; Ministry resources, Christian faith and life

A copy of this title is held at the National Library of New Zealand.

SWITCHED ON

A Discipleship Course for Children

Written by Sharline Aldridge

Dedicated to my grandchildren
Thaïs, Max, Oakley, Zoë, Laszlo

CONTENTS

To Parents and Caregivers,

My purpose in writing this book was to help my children and grandchildren to understand the basic beliefs in the Christian faith.

My hope is that you will find this book helpful too.

INTRODUCTION

To you my friend

This book is to share with you the most important thing you need to know in your life. It doesn't matter whether you are healthy or sick, have lots or little, are good looking or not, are good at school, sports, music, or art.

The only thing that matters is knowing and loving God. God wants you to be His friend.

God LOVES you.
God MADE you.
God KNOWS you.

God has a special plan for your life.
God created you to love and worship Him.
God is always with you, in good and bad times.
God promises never to leave you.
May you know God's presence throughout your life.
May you always seek to follow Him.
Be switched on to the things of God.

CHAPTER ONE

God Loves You

God loves you so very much.

No matter how you look, what you say or do.
He loves you heaps! And He always will.
Even if you turn away from Him, He still loves you
and wants to be your friend.
The Bible tells us this, over and over again,
just how much **God loves us.**

Romans 5:8

But God demonstrates His own love for us in this, while we were still sinners, Christ died for us.

Ephesians 3:18

...TO GRASP hOW WidE ANd LONG ANd
hiGh ANd dEEP iS ThE LOVE OF ChRiST.

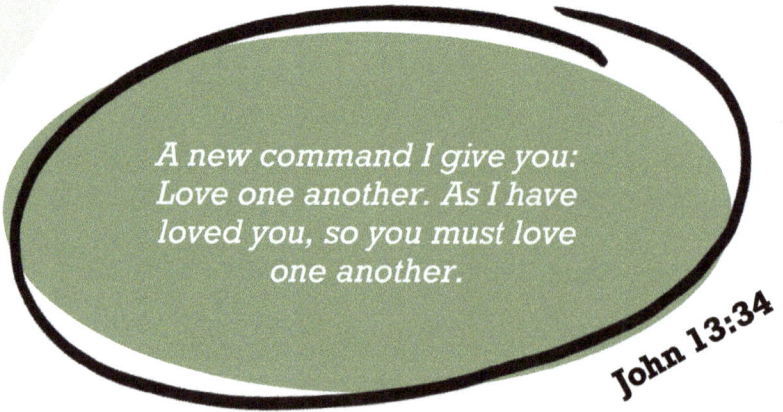

A new command I give you: Love one another. As I have loved you, so you must love one another.

John 13:34

4

You are special.

You are special because God made you. God says you are very valuable not because of anything you have said or done but **because of who you are.**

God cares about what happens to you every minute, every hour, every day, every month, and every year.

He planned the day you were born and the day you will die.
He made you and has a purpose for your life.
He placed you right where you are in the world for a reason.

Never forget the importance of your life in God's eyes.

*"For I know the plans
I have for you,"
declares the Lord,
"plans to prosper you
and not to harm you,
plans to give you
hope and a future."*

Jeremiah 29:11

CHAPTER TWO

God Made You

**In the Bible,
it tells us that God
created the world,
everything and
everyone in it.**

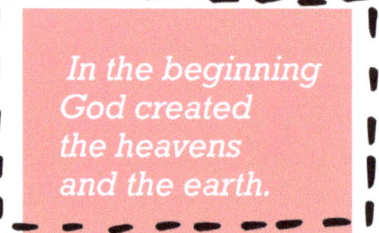

*In the beginning
God created
the heavens
and the earth.*

Genesis 1:1

*So God created man in His own
image, in the image of God
He created him; male and female
He created them.*

Genesis 1:27

God was happy with all He made.

God made you perfect. Even though you may think your nose
is too long, or your ears stick out, or you can't do this or that.
Remember God made you and He says in the Bible that
all He made is good.

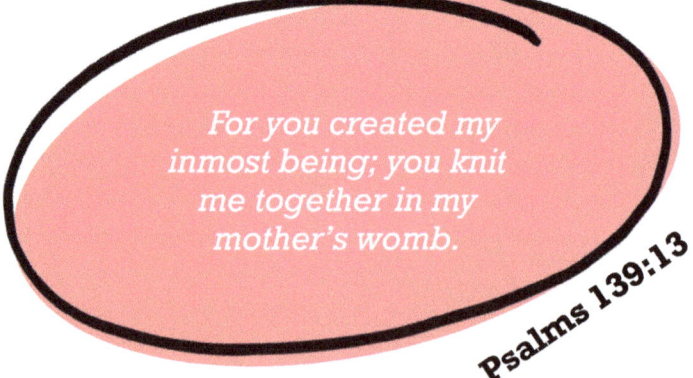

*For you created my
inmost being; you knit
me together in my
mother's womb.*

Psalms 139:13

8

The hands
that made the
twinkling stars,
made you.

The hands that made the
beautiful flowers, made you.
The hands that made the huge creatures
and the tiny insects, made you.
You are so special.

God made you and He never makes mistakes.

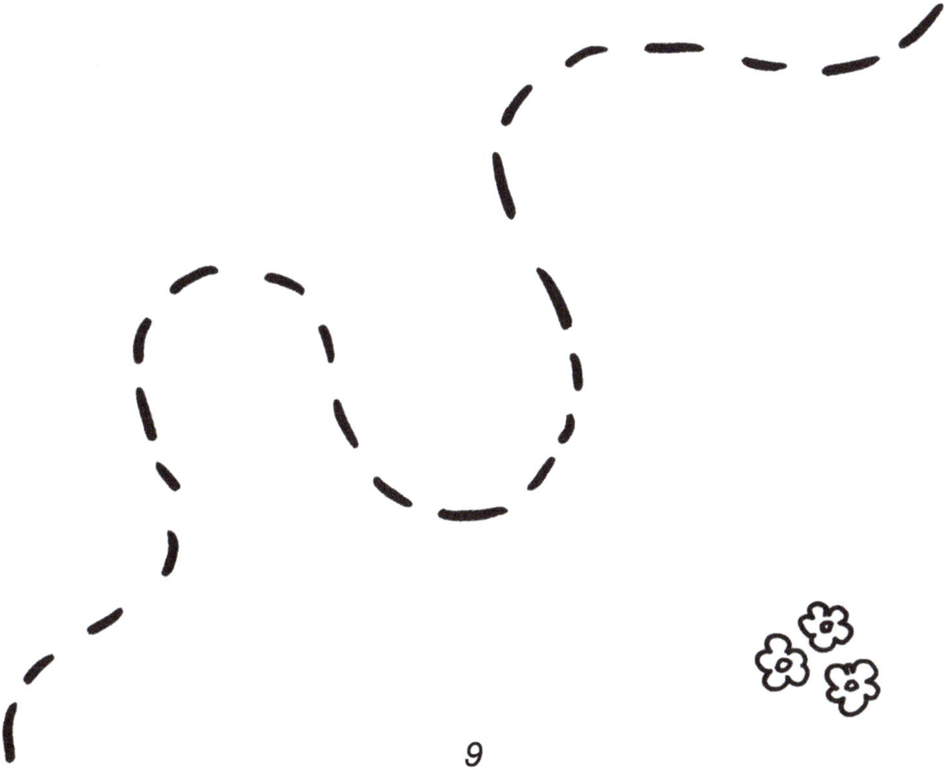

HE MADE YOU
THE WAY YOU
ARE FOR A
SPECIAL PURPOSE.

CHAPTER THREE

God Knows You

Because God made you,
He knows you the best.

He knows how you work. He knows how you feel.
He knows what makes you sad and mad and glad.

Oh Lord, you have searched me and you know me. You know when I sit and when I rise; you perceive my thoughts from afar. You discern my going out and my lying down; you are familiar with all my ways. Before a word is on my tongue, you know it completely, O Lord.

Psalm 139:1-4

God knows everything about you.
The words you speak,
the thoughts you think,
the number of hairs on your head.

And even the very hairs of your head are all numbered.

Matthew 10:30

12

CHAPTER FOUR

What the Bible Says I Am

What the Bible Says I Am

I am blessed coming in and going out .. Deuteronomy 28:6

I am the head and not the tail .... Deuteronomy 28:13

I am kept in safety .... Psalm 91:11

I am safe from the enemy .... Psalm 107:2

I am the salt of the earth .... Matthew 5:13

I am the light of the world .... Matthew 5:14

I am set free .... John 8:32

I am free from condemnation .... Romans 8:1

I am a child of God .... Romans 8:16

I am more than a conqueror .... Romans 8:37

I am victorious .... 1 Corinthians 15:57

I am a new creation .... 2 Corinthians 5:17

I am made rich in every way .... 2 Corinthians 9:11

I am blessed with all spiritual blessings .... Ephesians 1:3

I am holy and blameless in His sight .... Ephesians 1:4

I am saved from death .... Ephesians 2:5

I am strong in the Lord .... Ephesians 6:10

I am able to do all things .... Philippians 4:13

I am delivered from darkness .... Colossians 1:13

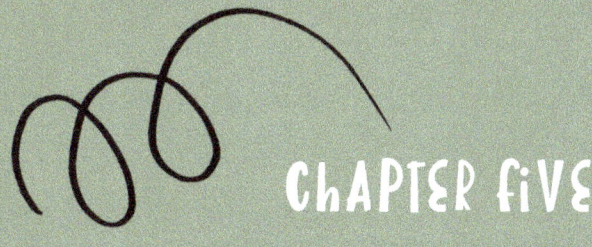

CHAPTER FIVE

Let's Talk About God

God is one but is made up of three parts.
The three parts are called the Trinity.

The three parts are:

1. **God the Father**

2. **God the Son – Jesus**

3. **God the Holy Spirit.**

This may be hard to understand.
An illustration to help you is H2O.
H2O can be water, ice, and steam.
H2O can therefore be liquid, solid, and gas.

Another way to understand the trinity,
is to think about your dad.
He can be father, a husband, a son,
a brother, a coach and a friend.
The same person can have different
names depending on where he is
and what he is doing.

Is there any other God?
There is no other God!

*I am the first and I am the last;
apart from me there is no God.*

Isaiah 44:6

16

Where is God?
He's everywhere!

Where can I go from your Spirit?
Where can I flee from your presence?
If I go up to the heavens, you are there;
if I make my bed in the depths, you are there.
If I rise on the wings of dawn, if I settle on the
far side of the sea, even there your hand will
guide me, your right hand will hold me fast.

Psalm 139:7-10

"AM I ONLY A GOd NEARbY?" dECLARES ThE LORd,
"ANd NOT A GOd FAR AWAY? CAN ANYONE hidE
iN SECRET PLACES SO ThAT I CANNOT SEE hiM?"

Jeremiah 23:23-24

What does God know?
He knows everything!

You know when I sit
and when I arise;
you perceive my
thoughts from afar.

Psalms 139:2

Nothing in all creation is
hidden from God's sight.
Everything is uncovered
and laid bare before the
eyes of Him...

Hebrews 4:13

17

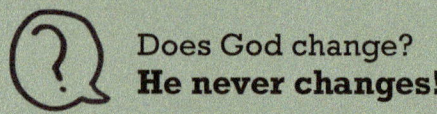 Does God change?
He never changes!

> # *Jesus Christ is the same yesterday and today and forever.*

Hebrews 13:8

 Is God's power limited?
God is all powerful!

Jeremiah 32:17

...you have made the heavens and the earth by your great power and outstretched arm. Nothing is too hard for you.

God is...

Holy - 1 Peter 1:16

Love - 1 John 4:8

Good - Psalm 100:5

Full of Wisdom - Psalm 104:24

Righteous and Just - Psalm 11:7

Faithful - Hebrews 10:23

Giver of Good Gifts - Matthew 7:7-11

Full of Grace - Ephesians 2:8

Loving and Full of Mercy - Ephesians 2:4-5

NAMES THAT DESCRIBE GOD

Lion of Judah

Immanuel

God Most High

King of Kings

Yahweh

Messiah

Creator

Redeemer

Ruler

Alpha and Omega

Friend

Abba

Light of the World

Rabbi

Prince of Peace

Beloved

The Way

Lord of Lords

Lord of All

Father

Jesus Christ

High Priest

Saviour

Bread of Life

God Almighty

Holy One

Teacher

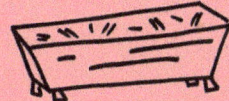

CHAPTER SIX

Let's Talk About Jesus

God became a human being in Jesus.

Jesus was a real person who lived over 2000 years ago. In fact our calendar years start when Jesus was born and we talk about years in relationship to Before Christ BC and from Jesus' birth AD. (AD stands for Anno Domini, which is Latin for "in the year of the Lord.") The stories of Jesus are found in the Bible in the books of Matthew, Mark, Luke and John.

In these books we read about His birth, the miracles He did, the things He taught, His death on the cross, and His rising from the dead. These books are eyewitness stories about Jesus by His closest friends who spent 3 years with Him. There are other stories about Jesus from historians living at this time too.

Although Jesus lived on earth only 33 years, He had a powerful impact. He lived a simple life on earth and experienced life with its joys and sadness. He never wrote a book, fought in a battle or built a city. **And yet Jesus is remembered, talked about and loved more than 2000 years later.**

What is one of Jesus' names and what does it mean?

Matthew 1:23

The virgin will be with child and will give birth to a son, and they will call him Immanuel, which means, 'God with us'.

Who is Jesus the image of?

> *He is the image of the invisible God, the firstborn over all creation. For by Him all things were created: things in heaven and on earth, visible and invisible, whether thrones or powers or rulers or authorities; all things were created by Him and for Him.*

Colossians 1:15-16

The Bible tells us who Jesus is.

Jesus is the Son of God	Matthew 3:17
Jesus is the Healer	Matthew 4:23-24
Jesus is the Teacher	Matthew 7:28-29
Jesus is the Friend of Sinners	Matthew 9:10-13
Jesus is the Messiah	John 1:41
Jesus is the Saviour of the world	John 3:16
Jesus is the Light of the World	John 8:12
Jesus is the Good Shepherd	John 10:11
Jesus is the Way, the Truth and the Life	John 14:6
Jesus is the Prince of Peace	John 14:27
Jesus is the Judge	Acts 10:42
Jesus is the Alpha and the Omega	Revelation 1:8
Jesus is the King of Kings	Revelations 19:16

Here are some things Jesus said:

> *"Love the Lord your God with all your heart and with all your soul and with all your mind. This is the first and greatest commandment. And the second is like it: Love your neighbour as yourself."*
> Matthew 22:37-39

> *"Do to others as you would have them do to you".*
> Luke 6:31

> *"With man this is impossible, but with God all things are possible."*
> Matthew 19:26

> *"For where your treasure is, there your heart will be also."*
> Matthew 6:21

> *"I am the way and the truth and the life. No one comes to the Father except through me."*
> John 14:6

> *"Let the little children come to me, and do not hinder them, for the kingdom of heaven belongs to such as these."*
> Matthew 19:14

 IF JESUS CAME AND LIVED HERE TODAY, WHAT WOULD HE SAY TO US?

CHAPTER SEVEN

Let's Talk About the Holy Spirit

God works His power through the Holy Spirit.

It is by the power of the Holy Spirit you are changed when you become a Christian. It is by the power of the Holy Spirit that God wants to fill you with Himself. We call this being 'filled with the Holy Spirit' or being 'baptised in the Holy Spirit.'

It's like being filled up with God. The Holy Spirit gives us strength and power to live the way God wants us to live. When we are tempted to do wrong, the Holy Spirit living in us helps us to do what is right. A car needs petrol for power to keep going, the Holy Spirit is God's power for us.

The Holy Spirit is a gift that God gives to all who believe in Him. There are other gifts that God gives us when we receive the Holy Spirit.

Some of these gifts are...

Faith - to help us believe

Healing - to pray for the sick

Wisdom - to know the right thing to do

Miracles - supernatural power in situations

Gift of Tongues - to help us pray

 How can you be filled with the Holy Spirit?
Ask God to fill you with the Holy Spirit.

> *"Do not leave Jerusalem, but wait for the gift my Father promised, which you have heard me speak about. For John baptised with water, but in a few days you will be baptised with the Holy Spirit."*

When Jesus left earth and returned to heaven, He gave the disciples the Holy Spirit at Pentecost. You can read this story in the Bible in Acts chapters 1 and 2.

Examples of people in the Bible who were filled with the Holy Spirit.

Joseph - Genesis 41:38
The Craftsmen - Exodus 31:1-5
Gideon - Judges 6:34
Samson - Judges 13:25 14:6
Saul - Acts 9:17-18
Jesus' disciples - Acts 2

CHAPTER EIGHT

What is a Christian?

What is religion?

Religion is people trying to find and please God
by their own efforts.

What is Christianity?

Christianity is God reaching down to us.
It is not made up or created by people.
It is a friendship with God.
Becoming a Christian means beginning
a relationship with God.

IT iS A GiFT FROM GOd.

You can't buy it or earn it. It is a decision to love God and let
Him become the most important thing in your life.

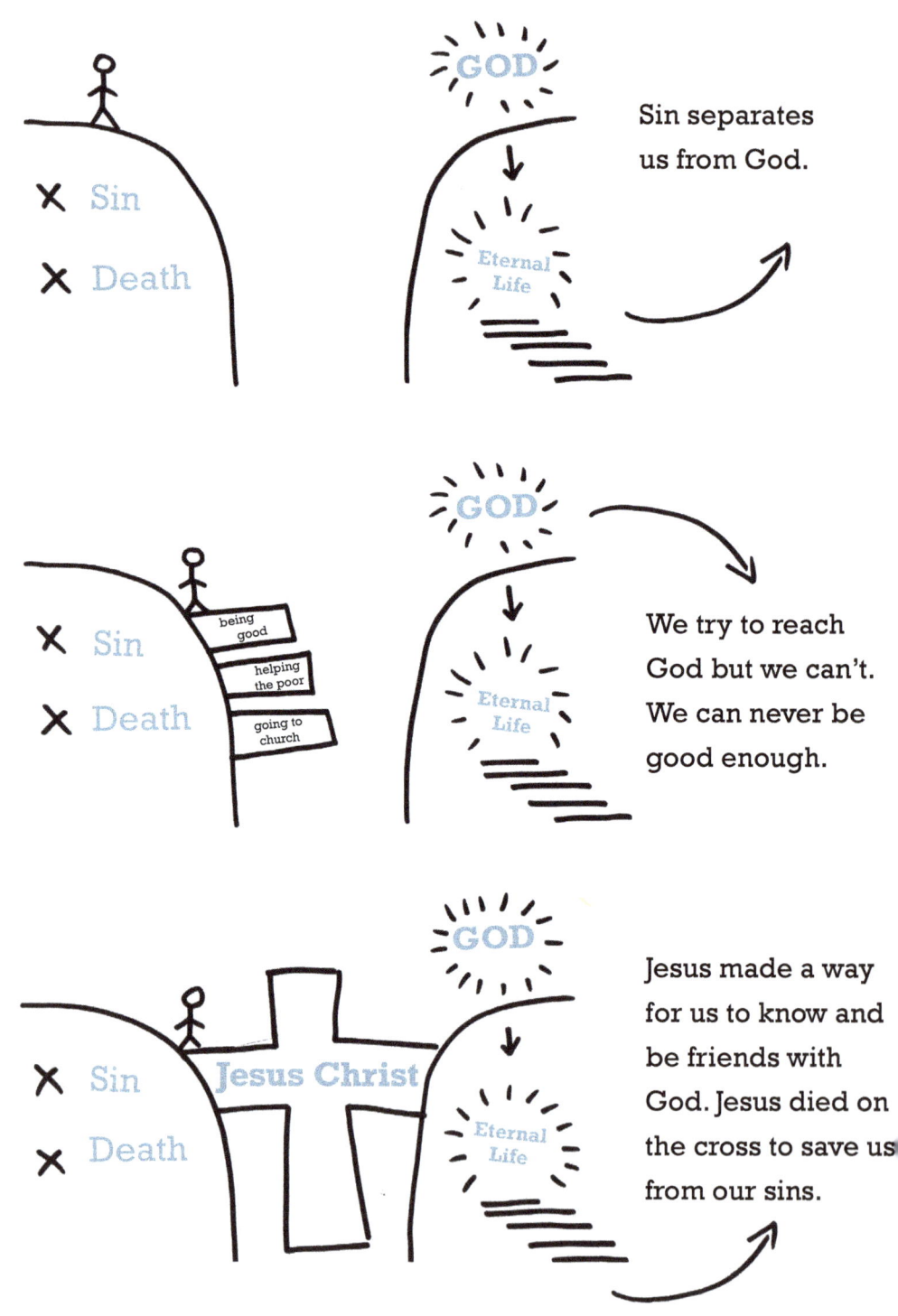

Sin separates us from God.

We try to reach God but we can't. We can never be good enough.

Jesus made a way for us to know and be friends with God. Jesus died on the cross to save us from our sins.

CHAPTER NINE

What is Sin?

Sin is anything you say, do or think that goes against what God wants.

The Bible says that we have all sinned and therefore we are separated from God. We cannot be friends with God, until we say sorry for our sins and let God forgive us.

...for all have sinned and fall short of the glory of God...

Romans 3:23

← 1 John 1:9 →

IF WE CONFESS OUR SINS, HE IS FAITHFUL AND JUST AND WILL FORGIVE US OUR SINS AND PURIFY US FROM ALL UNRIGHTEOUSNESS.

...and the blood of Jesus, His Son, purifies us from all sin.

1 John 1:7

The cross is important to Christians because Jesus paid the price by dying on the cross to save us from our sins. He took the punishment for the wrong things we have done so that He could have a relationship with us.

Once you have asked Jesus to come into your life,
He cleanses you from all your sins and you can start a
friendship with Him. You don't have to keep asking Him to
come in. You will sin at times and need to ask Him to forgive
you again. But He will always be with you if you continue to
live your life for Him.

Who can become a Christian?
EVERYONE! Big/small, young/old, all of us!

*For God so loved the world
that He gave His one and
only Son, that whoever
believes in Him shall not
perish but have eternal life.*

John 3:16

How do you become a Christian?

> *...If you confess with your mouth, "Jesus is Lord", and believe in your heart that God raised Him from the dead, you will be saved.*

Romans 10:9

John 5:24

I TELL YOU ThE TRUTh, WhOEVER hEARS MY WORd ANd bELiEVES HiM WhO SENT ME hAS ETERNAL LifE ANd WiLL NOT bE CONdEMNEd, hE hAS CROSSEd OVER fROM dEATh TO LifE.

To become a Christian the Bible talks about believing in Jesus. Deciding to be a Christian is saying, "I need Jesus in my life and from now on I want to live a life that pleases Him." You can pray wherever you are and ask Jesus to come into your life and be your Saviour and Lord.

Here is a prayer you can say to ask Jesus into your life.

Dear Jesus,

Thank you for dying on the cross for me. Forgive me for all the things I have done wrong that separate me from knowing you. Come into my life. I want to live my life for you. Help me to follow you every day. Thank you that you love me and have a plan for my life.

Amen

 HAVE YOU ASKEd JESUS TO COME iNTO YOUR LifE? DO YOU WANT TO FOLLOW JESUS?

How do you know you are a Christian?

God is wanting to come into your life.

If you ask Him in, the Bible says He comes in. The choice is yours. When you ask Jesus to come into your life, you may feel different. Sometimes people cry or feel joy or peace. You will have a desire to learn more about God.

Here I am! I stand at the door and knock. If anyone hears my voice and opens the door, I will come in and eat with him, and he with me.

Revelation 3:20

YET TO ALL WHO RECEIVE HIM, TO THOSE WHO BELIEVED IN HIS NAME, HE GAVE THE RIGHT TO BECOME CHILDREN OF GOD.

John 1:12

CHAPTER TEN

Growing in the things of God

It is good to have friends.

It's good to get together with friends to talk and have fun. It takes time to get to know someone and often the best things you remember in life, are the good times with friends.

When you become a Christian, it is like starting a friendship with God. **He will be the best friend you have ever had!**

Just like a friend, you need to spend time with God to get to know Him. The best way of doing this is by reading the Bible and talking to Him in prayer. God speaks to us through the Bible, and we speak to Him in prayer. Decide today to spend time with God every day and let Him become your best friend.

Four things that will help you to grow in the things of God are:

1. Read the Bible - God's Word

2. Prayer - talking and listening to God

3. Going to Church

4. Sharing with others about God

1. Read the Bible - God's Word

The Bible is the Word of God. It is not just an ordinary book. God inspired men to write it. Every word is truth and filled with God's power and authority. The Bible is our manual on how God intended us to live.

The Bible gives us instructions and helps us understand God and His plan for our life. It encourages us and it guides us. God will speak to us and guide us if we read and study the Bible.

Throughout the world and for over 2000 years, the Bible has been relevant to different cultures and generations by giving instruction, hope, and knowledge of God.

THAT'S TOTALLY AMAZING AND INCREDIBLE!

Reading the Bible
helps
us
to
grow in the things of God.

Just like we need to feed our physical body, we need to feed our spiritual body with the Word of God.

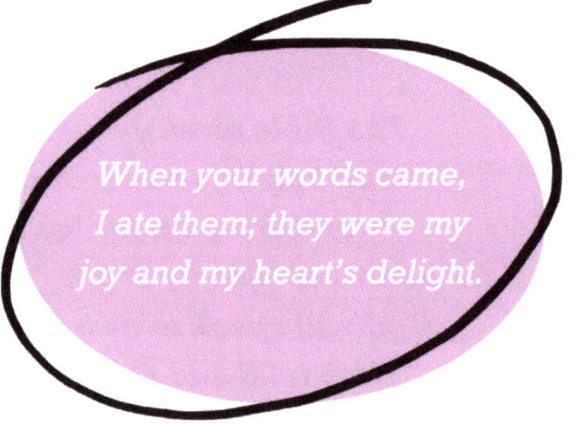

When your words came, I ate them; they were my joy and my heart's delight.

Jeremiah 15:16

ALL SCRIPTURE iS GOd bREAThEd ANd iS USEFUL FOR TEAChiNG, REbUKiNG, CORRECTiNG ANd TRAiNiNG iN RiGhTEOUSNESS, SO ThAT ThE MAN OF GOd MAY bE ThOROUGhLY EQUiPPEd FOR EVERY GOOd WORK.

2 Timothy 3:16-17

HAVE YOU GOT A BibLE ThAT YOU CAN REAd?
DO YOU NEEd SOMEONE TO REAd iT WiTh YOU?

The Word of God will guide you.

Your word is a lamp to my feet and a light for my path.

- Psalm 119:105

The Word of God will help you live a life without sin.

How can a young man keep his way pure?
By living according to your Word.

- Psalm 119:9

The Word of God will help you live well.

Do not let this Book of the Law depart from your mouth; meditate on it day and night, so that you may be careful to do everything written in it. Then you will be prosperous and successful.

- Joshua 1:8

The Word of God will give you freedom.

I will always obey your law forever and ever. I will walk about in freedom for I have sought out your precepts.

- Psalm 119:44-45

The Word of God will give life and health to your body.

My son, pay attention to what I say, listen closely to my words. Do not let them out of your sight, keep them within your heart; for they are life to those who find them and health to a man's whole body.

- Proverbs 4:20-22

The Word of God will make you wise.

Your commands make me wiser than my enemies.

- Psalm 119:98

How to read the Bible

I like to read the Bible every day. Sometimes I read just 1 or 2 verses and sometimes I read a whole chapter.

I have a notebook which sometimes:

▷ I write down verses I like

▷ I draw a picture of what I have read

▷ I imagine myself in the story

▷ I pray and ask God to speak to me through these verses

▷ I think about what these verses teach me about Jesus and how to live my life

▷ If I don't understand what I have read, I ask someone to explain it to me

It is good to start reading the New Testament first.

2. Prayer – Talking and Listening to God

Prayer is talking and listening to God. And most of us love to talk!
It would be crazy to invite a friend over to your house and then
not talk to them. God is our friend and He loves us to talk to Him.
Anytime, anywhere you can talk to Him.

You don't have to be in church to talk to Him or close your
eyes. He's always with you and keen to hear from you.
Prayer is like talking to a friend. You talk and you listen.
This is how prayer should be.

**Take time throughout the day
to talk and listen to God.**

Does God really hear me when I pray?

*The Lord is far from the wicked but he hears the prayer
of the righteous.*
- Proverbs 15:29

*This is the confidence we have in approaching God: that if we
ask anything according to His will, He hears us.
And if we know that He hears us - whatever we ask, we know
that we have what we ask of Him.*
- 1 John 5:14-15

What pleases God?

*The Lord detests the sacrifice of the wicked
but the prayer of the upright pleases Him.*
- 1 Thessalonians 5:17-18

How do I pray?

+ Thank Him – He's done so much for you.

Pray continually; give thanks in all circumstances,
for this is God's will for you in Christ Jesus.
- **Proverbs 15:8**

+ Praise Him – He's a great God.

I will extol the Lord at all times;
His praise will always be on
my lips.
- **Psalm 34:1**

+ Say sorry for the things you have done wrong.

If we confess our sins, He is faithful and just and will forgive
us our sins and purify us from all unrighteousness.
- **1 John 1:9**

+ Pray for others who have needs.

I urge, then, first of all, that requests, prayers, intercession
and thanksgiving be made for everyone, for kings and all
those in authority.
- **1 Timothy 2:1-2**

+ Pray for your needs and concerns.

Ask and it will be given to you; seek and you will find;
knock and the door will be opened to you. For everyone
who asks receives; he who seeks finds; and to him who knocks,
the door will be opened.
- **Matthew 7:7-8**

God hears our prayers

He also has a plan for us. Sometimes we can pray for things that aren't in God's plan. I heard someone say once that God always answers our prayers.

God either says...

"YES that's just what I want to happen"

or He says

"Hey, I've got a better idea".

> *...each one had a harp and they were holding golden bowls full of incense, which are the prayers of the saints.*

Revelations 5:8

In this verse it says that angels bring our prayers to God in golden bowls. How precious our prayers must be to God.

Stories in the Bible about prayer:

Elijah > 1 Kings 17:19-21
Daniel > Daniel 6:10
Jesus talking about Prayer > Matthew 6:6
The Lord's Prayer > Matthew 6:9-13
Jesus > Mark 6:46 > Luke 5:16 > Luke 6:12
Peter > Acts 10:9
Cornelius > Acts 10:30
Early Church > Acts 12:5
Elijah > James 5:17

The Lord's Prayer

In the Bible Jesus teaches His friends how to pray. Often this prayer is said in churches.

Our Father who is in heaven,
hallowed be Your name,
Your kingdom come,
Your will be done
on earth as it is in heaven.
Give us today our daily bread.
Forgive us our sins,
as we forgive those
who sin against us.
Lead us not into temptation,
but deliver us from evil.
For Yours is the kingdom,
the power and the glory.
Forever and ever, Amen.

Matthew 6:9-13

WHAT CAN YOU THANK GOD FOR TODAY?
WHAT DO YOU NEED HELP WITH?
SPEAK TO GOD AND SHARE YOUR NEEDS.

3. Going to Church

The church is a group of people who love God and come together to pray, worship, study the Word of God - the Bible, and care for each other. A church can meet in a house, a building, a school, outside under a tree, at a cafe or anywhere.

CHURCH IS NOT A BUILDING BUT A GROUP OF PEOPLE WHO LOVE GOD.

It is good to go to a church that you like and that teaches from the Bible. At church you can learn about God, be supported and encouraged by others. At church you can share things you don't understand about the Bible and help others Christians learn about God.

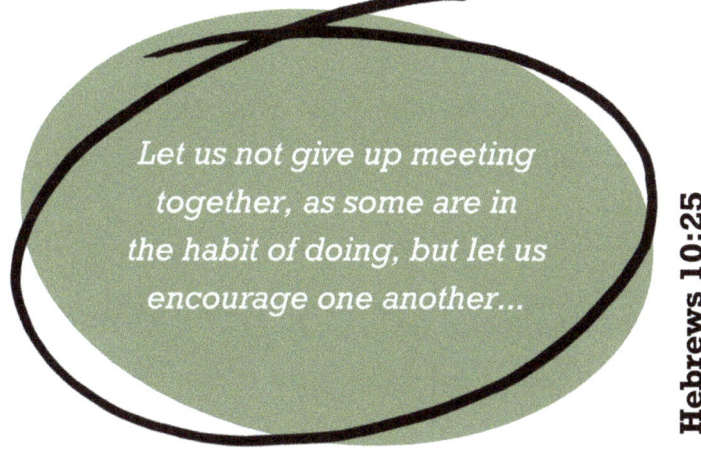

Let us not give up meeting together, as some are in the habit of doing, but let us encourage one another...

Hebrews 10:25

47

...Love one another.
As I have loved you,
so you must love one another.
By this all men will know
that you are my disciples,
if you love one another.

John 13:34-35

EVERY DAY THEY CONTINUED TO MEET TOGETHER IN THE TEMPLE COURTS. THEY BROKE BREAD IN THEIR HOMES AND ATE TOGETHER WITH GLAD AND SINCERE HEARTS, PRAISING GOD.

Acts 2:46 (the first church)

IS THERE A CHURCH NEARBY THAT YOU COULD GO TO? WHAT'S THE BEST THING ABOUT YOUR CHURCH?

4. Telling Others About Jesus

Jesus is Good News. We love talking to people about things. We share with our friends about good movies we have seen, funny books we have read, food we like to eat, and our opinions.

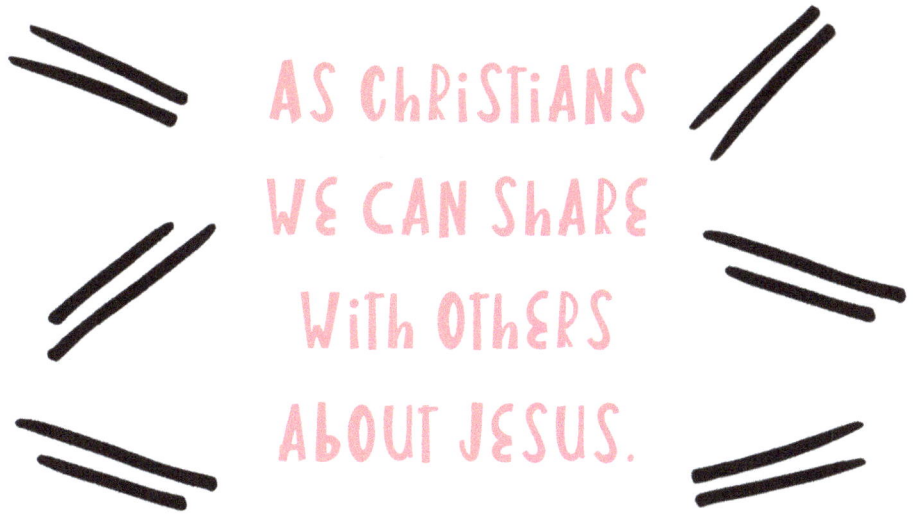

AS CHRISTIANS WE CAN SHARE WITH OTHERS ABOUT JESUS.

Don't be shy to tell others about Jesus. You will have friends who are eager to know about Jesus. You don't have to know everything about Him before you share your faith with others. Often people who know you are a Christian may ask you questions about God. If you don't know all the answers, go and ask a parent or leader at the church or pray and ask God to reveal the answer to you. Some people may laugh or tease you because you are a Christian. **Pray for them so that they too may find God.**

If you confess with your mouth, "Jesus is Lord", and believe in your heart that God raised Him from the dead, you will be saved.

Romans 10:9

The Fruit of the Spirit
God wants us to grow in...

PATIENCE

LOVE

GOODNESS

FAITHFULNESS

JOY

PEACE

KINDNESS

These are characteristics that God wants us to grow in our lives.
They are found in Galatians 5:22-23.

CHAPTER ELEVEN

Sharing The Good News

Here is a way to share the Good News about God to others.

Just remember the five colours...

 **Gold is for holy.** God is holy and perfect. He loves you and He made you. He didn't make you like a puppet. He gave you the choice whether to love Him or not.

 **Black is for sin.** We are all born with sin. Sin separates us from God. It says in the Bible that "all have sinned" Romans 3:23. Yet God still wants to be our friend.

 **Red is for blood.** God sent Jesus to take the punishment for our sin. He died on the cross and shed His blood to take away our sin.

 **White is for clean.** To be right before God, you can ask Jesus to forgive your sins and to come into your life. This makes you clean before God.

 **Green is for growing.** When you ask Jesus to come into your life, you can grow in the things of God by reading the Bible, praying, and going to church. All these things will help you grow as a Christian.

CHAPTER TWELVE

Communion

Communion is remembering and celebrating

the sacrifice Jesus made for us when He died on the cross to save us from our sins. Some churches have communion every Sunday and some once a month. Communion is a quiet and thoughtful time at church. We must show respect when we take communion.

What happens at Communion?

First a small talk is given to remind us that Jesus died for us on the cross. The night before Jesus died on the cross, He had a meal with His disciples. He gave them wine and bread. This is called the Last Supper. The wine represents Jesus' blood and the bread represents Jesus' body.

JESUS SAid "dO ThiS
TO REMEMbER ME ANd
WhAT I hAVE dONE fOR YOU."

Then small glasses of grape juice or wine and small pieces of bread are given to everyone who wants to take communion. At some churches, everyone will drink the juice and eat the bread at the same time. At some churches, people drink the juice and eat the bread in their own time. At some churches, people go up the front and the pastor or priest gives out the bread and wine.

Before you drink the juice or eat the bread, it is good to say a special prayer of thanks to God and to ask forgiveness if you know there is sin in your life.

While they were eating, Jesus took bread, gave thanks and broke it, and gave it to His disciples, saying, "Take and eat; this is my body." Then He took the cup, gave thanks and offered it to them, saying, "Drink from it, all of you. This is my blood of the covenant, which is poured out for many for the forgiveness of sins."

Matthew 26:26-28

CHAPTER THIRTEEN

Baptism

When a person becomes a new President or Prime Minister of a country there is often a special ceremony that takes place. This usually happens after they become the new leader and it is a public declaration of their new position. The leader declares and promises that they will do certain things and it is a time of great celebration.

When someone becomes a Christian, they too can decide to make a public announcement by being baptised.

Getting baptised is like declaring to everyone that they are a follower of Jesus and that they are living a life pleasing to Him. It is a great time of celebration for that person. In the Bible, many people who became Christians were baptised in water.

Why do we need to be baptised?

Jesus was baptised. He tells us to go and tell others about Him and to baptise those who believe. The word baptise comes from the Greek word 'Baptizo' which mean to dip, to plunge, to immerse.

> *Therefore go and make disciples of all nations, baptising them in the name of the Father and of the Son and of the Holy Spirit...*
>
> **Matthew 28:19-20**

What does being baptised mean?

Baptism is like a picture of the death and resurrection of Jesus. We put our past to death by going into the water, and when we rise out of the water, we are made new. ***It is a public declaration of faith in Jesus and an act of obedience.***

Who can be baptised?

People who have asked Jesus to come into their lives and want to follow Jesus. The Bible doesn't say anything about age but a person must be able to understand the importance of it.

BUT WHEN THEY BELIEVED PHILIP AS HE PREACHED THE GOOD NEWS OF THE KINGDOM OF GOD AND THE NAME OF JESUS CHRIST, THEY WERE BAPTISED, BOTH MEN AND WOMEN.

Acts 8:12

What if I have already been baptised when I was a baby?

A baby being sprinkled with water is a sign that the parents want God to bless their child. We believe that a person needs to have chosen to follow God before they are baptised. A baby has not made this choice.

Stories of people who were baptised in the Bible are:

Jesus . . . Matthew 3:13-17
Lydia . . . Acts 16:13-15
The jailer and his family . . . Acts 16:22-34
The eunuch of Ethiopia . . . Acts 8:26-39

 **Would you like to be baptised?**

CHAPTER FOURTEEN

Our Enemy – Satan

Satan is the opposite of all God is.

He was a high ranking angel who became an evil enemy of God. There was a cosmic war in heaven as Satan tried to become God. But God and His angels won the war and Satan was evicted from heaven. It is assumed that the angels who followed Satan became demons and evil spirits.

To know more about this, read Ezekiel 28:1-19 and Isaiah 14:12-17.

Some names of Satan in the Bible:

Serpent | Isaiah 27:1
Tempter | Matthew 4:3
Evil One | Matthew 13:19
Devil, Murderer, Father of Lies | John 8:44
Thief | John 10:10
Prince of this World | John 12:31
Lawless One | 2 Thessalonians 2:8
The Devil | 1 Peter 5:8
The Beast | Revelation 11:7

What does Satan do?

The Bible tells us that Satan comes to steal, kill and destroy. He is the father of lies and wants us to worship him instead of God.

John 10:10

JESUS SAID..."THE THIEF COMES ONLY TO STEAL AND KILL AND DESTROY; I HAVE COME THAT THEY MAY HAVE LIFE, AND HAVE IT TO THE FULL."

John 8:44

...for he is a liar and the father of lies.

The god of this age has blinded the minds of unbelievers, so that they cannot see the light of the gospel...

2 Corinthians 4:4

2 Timothy 2:26

..AND THAT THEY WILL COME TO THEIR SENSES AND ESCAPE FROM THE TRAP OF THE DEVIL, WHO HAS TAKEN THEM CAPTIVE TO DO HIS WILL.

How do we protect ourselves from Satan?

Ask God to help you to be strong and grow in the things of God. Read the Bible and spend time with God praying and listening to Him. Stay away from things that may tempt you away from doing what God wants you to do.

SUBMIT YOURSELVES, THEN, TO GOD. RESIST THE DEVIL, AND HE WILL FLEE FROM YOU.
COME NEAR TO GOD AND HE WILL COME NEAR TO YOU.

James 4:7-8

Be strong in the Lord and in His mighty power.
Put on the full armour of God so that you can take your stand against the devil's schemes.

Ephesians 6:10-11

BE SELF-CONTROLLED AND ALERT. YOUR ENEMY THE DEVIL PROWLS AROUND LIKE A ROARING LION LOOKING FOR SOMEONE TO DEVOUR. RESIST HIM STANDING FIRM IN THE FAITH...

1 Peter 5:8-9

Who wins the battle - God or Satan?

In the Bible, it tells us that God will defeat Satan,
that God has won the war over sin and death. **YAY!**

AND THE dEViL, WHO dECEiVEd THEM,
WAS THROWN iNTO THE LAKE OF bURNiNG SULFUR...
THEY WiLL bE TORMENTEd dAY ANd NiGHT
FOR EVER ANd EVER.

Revelation 20:10

Hell is where Satan lives.

It is a horrible place of suffering and evil.

*They will throw them into the blazing furnace,
where there will be weeping and gnashing of teeth.*

Matthew 13:41-42

The Armour of God

In Ephesians 6:11-17 it tells us to put on the armour of God so that we can fight the enemy Satan.

We need...

The helmet of salvation
– is knowing that Jesus has saved us and
   He protects our mind from lies of the enemy.

The shield of faith
– is our faith in God to protect us from doubt
   and worries from the enemy.

The shoes of peace
– is going out and sharing the Good News of Jesus.

The sword of the Spirit
– is God's Word, the Bible, which we use to fight
   our enemy.

The breastplate of righteousness
– is to protect us from attacks from our enemy,
   helping us to do what is right.

The belt of truth
– is the certainty and support in knowing
   the truth of God.

Helmet of Salvation

Breastplate of Righteousness

Sword of the Spirit

Shield of Faith

Belt of Truth

Shoes of Peace

CHAPTER FIFTEEN

The Bible

The Bible is a book that tells us about God.

It is God's Word. It shows us what He is like, what He has done, and what He wants us to do. It tells us about ourselves, about how God made us and about how sin came into the world. It tells us about Jesus, who came to show us how much God loves us and wants to forgive our sins. **The Bible is telling one big story about God and His love for us.**

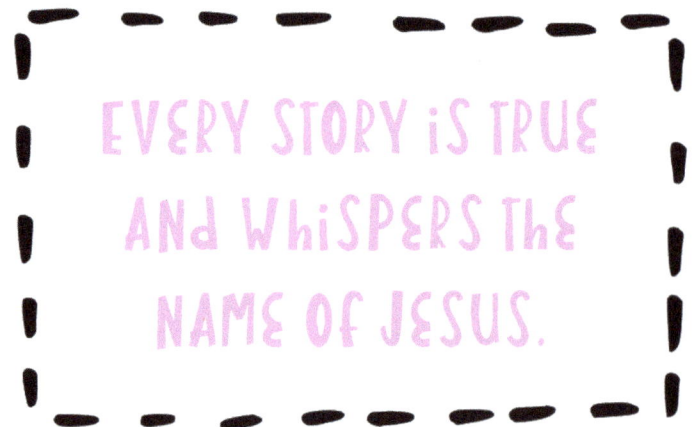

EVERY STORY iS TRUE AND WhiSPERS ThE NAME OF JESUS.

Who wrote the Bible?

God inspired around 35 different people to write down what He wanted us to know. God let each writer use his own personality and style. The people who wrote the Bible lived a long time ago. Some, like Moses, lived as long as 3500 years ago. Others, like John, lived about 2000 years ago. In lots of ways they were just like we are. People who had doubts, people who did right and wrong things. God used them to write down words that tell us about Him and His love for us.

Facts about the Bible

The word Bible comes from a Greek word Biblia which means books. Picking up a Bible is like picking up a stack of books. There are 66 books in the Bible. It is sort of like picking up a library. There are more than 35 authors, which include a tax collector, a doctor, and a shepherd.

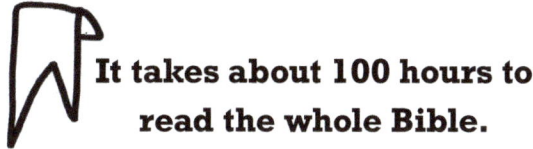 **It takes about 100 hours to read the whole Bible.**

The Bible is divided into 2 main sections:

OLD TESTAMENT   NEW TESTAMENT

The Old Testament was written telling us things that happened before Jesus came to earth.
The New Testament was written telling us things about when Jesus was on earth and after He left.

Each book in the Bible is broken into parts called chapters. Each chapter is broken into short sections called verses. All the verses are numbered so it is easy to find your way around the Bible.

◀ Shortest Verse

The shortest verse is John 11:35.

"Jesus wept".

◀ Longest Chapter

The longest chapter in the Bible is Psalm 119.

It has 176 verses.

◀ Longest Book

The book of Psalms is the longest book in the Bible.

It is like a hymn book.

It has 150 hymns or prayers in it.

◀ Shortest Book

John wrote some books in the New Testament. One of them is 2 John. **It has only 13 verses, which makes it the shortest book in the Bible.**

The grass withers and the flowers fall, but the Word of our God stands forever.

Isaiah 40:8

The First Book in the Bible

The first book in the Bible is Genesis. It tells us about when the world was created and it tells us of special promises God made to man. It shows us that God loves us and has a plan for our lives and He wants us to know Him. Here is the first verse in the Bible....

GENESIS 1:1

*In the beginning,
God created the heavens
and the earth.*

The Last Book in the Bible

The last book in the Bible is Revelation. It is about the last days before Jesus Christ returns to earth. John wrote this book after God gave him a vision. It teaches us that in evil times, God is still in control.

Here is the last verse in the Bible...

REVELATIONS 22:21

*The grace of the Lord Jesus
be with God's people. Amen.*

FAMOUS BIBLE STORIES

START READING THE BIBLE IN THE NEW TESTAMENT. READ THE STORIES OF JESUS IN MATTHEW, MARK, LUKE AND JOHN. THESE STORIES ABOUT JESUS ARE EASY TO UNDERSTAND.

CHAPTER SIXTEEN

The Commandments

In the Old Testament God gave the people of Israel 10 commandments or important laws.

Over the years these 10 commandments have become part of the laws in many countries. **These are important guidelines given to us by God on how to live.**

The Ten Commandments are found in Exodus 20:2-17.

1. Do not have other gods besides the one true God.

2. Do not make an idol to worship.

3. Do not misuse the name of the Lord your God.

4. Keep the Sabbath day holy.

5. Honour your father and your mother.

6. Do not murder.

7. Keep your marriage promises.

8. Do not steal.

9. Do not lie.

10. Do not want things that belong to someone else.

CHAPTER SEVENTEEN

Heaven

**The Bible talks about heaven over 600 times.
It doesn't answer all our questions but it does tell us....**

Heaven is where God lives.
Look down from heaven, your holy dwelling place, and bless your people...
- **Deuteronomy 26:15**

Heaven is where angels live.
When the angels had left them and gone into heaven...
- **Luke 2:15**

Heaven is where those who love God will go when they die.
Jesus says in the Bible that he is preparing a place for those who trust and believe in Him.

*Do not let your hearts be troubled.
Trust in God; trust also in me.
In my Father's house are many rooms...
I am going there to prepare a place for you.*

John 14:1-2

Those who believe and love God when they die, go straight to heaven.

When Jesus was on the cross, He spoke to a criminal who was being crucified as well. Jesus said to him...

{ "I TELL YOU ThE TRUTh, TOdAY YOU WiLL bE WiTh ME iN PARAdiSE."
Luke 23:43 }

Life
in
heaven
is
forever.

John 3:15

"...that everyone who believes in Him may have eternal life."

What does the Bible say Heaven is like?

In Revelation it tells us 5 NO MORES about heaven. There will be...

 NO MORE TEARS

 NO MORE dEATh

 NO MORE SAdNESS

 NO MORE CRYiNG

 NO MORE PAiN.

> *He will wipe every tear from their eyes. There will be no more death or mourning or crying or pain, for the old order of things has passed away.*

Revelation 21:4

The Bible also tells us that heaven is a spectacular city of great beauty.

Revelation 21:21

The twelve gates were twelve pearls, each gate made of a single pearl. The great street of the city was of pure gold, like transparent glass.

IT SHONE WITH THE GLORY OF GOd, ANd iTS bRiLLiANCE WAS LiKE ThAT OF A VERY PRECiOUS jEWEL, LiKE jASPER, CLEAR AS CRYSTAL.

Revelation 21:11

People from every country will be in heaven.

...I LOOKEd ANd THERE bEFORE ME WAS A GREAT MULTiTUdE ThAT NO ONE COULd COUNT, FROM EVERY NATiON, TRibE, PEOPLE ANd LANGUAGE, STANdiNG bEFORE ThE ThRONE...

Revelation 7:9

The Bible doesn't answer all our questions about heaven.

It tells us we will have new and perfect bodies that won't age or become sick, weak or die.

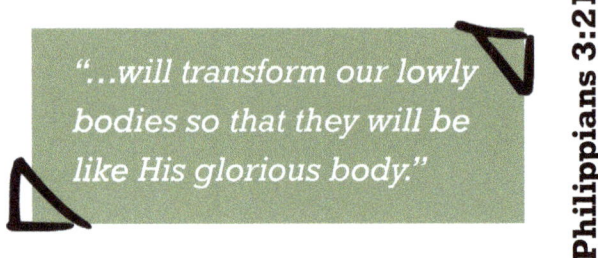

"...will transform our lowly bodies so that they will be like His glorious body."

Philippians 3:21

If we believe and love God, we do not need to fear death

+ **We know that we will be with Him.**

+ **We know He is preparing a place for us in heaven.**

+ **We know that heaven is an awesome place.**

CHAPTER EIGHTEEN

When Jesus Returns

The Bible tells us that one day Jesus will return to earth. This time He will come not as a baby but as a King, a Ruler, and Judge.

...They will see the Son of Man coming on the clouds of the sky, with power and great glory.

Matthew 24:30

Look, He is coming
with the clouds and
every eye will see Him...
"I am the Alpha and Omega,"
says the Lord God,
"who is and who was
and who is to come,
the Almighty."

Revelation 1:7-8

The Bible tells us that there will be a time on earth when the world will be out of control. There will be earthquakes, famines, wars, and diseases.

YOU WILL hEAR OF WARS AND RUMOURS OF WARS, bUT SEE TO iT THAT YOU ARE NOT ALARMED...

Matthew 24:6-7

THERE WILL BE TERRIBLE TIMES IN THE LAST DAYS.
PEOPLE WILL BE LOVERS OF THEMSELVES, LOVERS OF
MONEY, BOASTFUL, PROUD, ABUSIVE, DISOBEDIENT TO
THEIR PARENTS, UNGRATEFUL, UNHOLY, WITHOUT LOVE,
UNFORGIVING, SLANDEROUS, WITHOUT SELF-CONTROL...

The end of time can seem like a scary and frightening time to be alive. But God has told us in the Bible what is to come and God knows what He is doing. God is in control. He wins the war between good and evil. **We do not need to be afraid.**

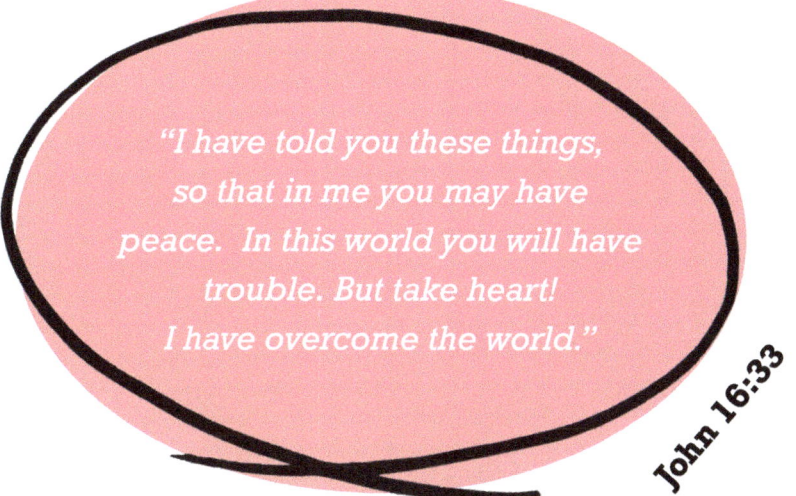

"I have told you these things, so that in me you may have peace. In this world you will have trouble. But take heart! I have overcome the world."

John 16:33

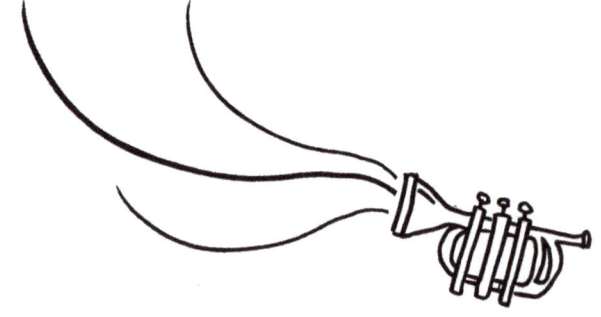

*For the Lord himself will
come down from heaven,
with a loud command,
with the voice of the archangel
and with the trumpet call of God,
and the dead in Christ will rise first.
After that, we who are still alive
and are left will be caught up
together with them in the clouds
to meet the Lord in the air.
And so we will be
with the Lord forever.*

1 Thessalonians 4:16-17

CHAPTER NINETEEN

Great Bible Verses to Learn

When I was a child I learnt many Bible verses.
Whenever I am scared, I remember the verse, **"I will never leave you or forsake you"** (Hebrews 13:5). Or when I want to give up on something difficult, I remember the verse, **"I can do all things through Christ who strengthens me"** (Philippians 4:13). Memorising Bible verses helps me focus on God and reminds me of God's love and care for me.

Here are some verses which you may like to learn.

> *For God so loved the world*
> *that He gave His only Son,*
> *that whosoever believes*
> *in Him should not perish*
> *but have everlasting life.*
> (John 3:16)

If God is for us,
who can be against us?
(Romans 8:31)

I will never leave you
or forsake you.
(Hebrews 13:5)

While we were
still sinners,
Christ died for us.
(Romans 5:8)

He has showed you, O man, what is good and what does the Lord require of you? To act justly, to love mercy and to walk humbly with your God.
(Micah 6:8)

Great is the Lord and most worthy of praise; His greatness no one can fathom.
(Psalms 145:3)

No eye has seen, no ear has heard, no mind has conceived, what God has prepared for those who love Him.
(1 Corinthians 2:9)

I can do all things through Christ who strengthens me.
(Philippians 4:13)

For God has not given us a spirit of fear, but of power and love and of sound mind.
(2 Timothy 1:7)

CHAPTER TWENTY

Your Story

There will be times you may like to tell your story or testimony.

This is your story about the things that God is doing in your life. In children's church or with some friends, you may like to talk about how and when you became a Christian.
Your testimony will encourage others.

Here is an outline you can use to write your testimony.

Hi, my name is _____

I am _____ (years old)

I live in _____

I go to _____ (school)

I became a Christian _____ (when)

The reason I became a Christian

_____

_____

My favourite Bible verse is

_____

I love God because

_____

 **WhO CAN YOU ShARE ThiS WiTh?**

FiNAL ThOUGhTS

God LOVES you.
God MADE you.
God KNOWS you.

God has a special plan for your life. God created you to love and worship Him. He is always with you. God promises never to leave you. Life is not always easy. But God loves you and He will guide and lead you.

Spend time with God reading the Bible.
Talk and listen to God in prayer.
Make decisions according to the Bible because the Bible is our manual to live a life for God.
Be 'Switched On' to the things of God!

The Lord bless you
and keep you.
the Lord make His face
shine on you
and be gracious to you;
the Lord turn
His face toward you
and give you peace.

Numbers 6:24-26

www.ingramcontent.com/pod-product-compliance
Lightning Source LLC
Chambersburg PA
CBHW051339120626
46547CB00016B/2615